ONE
PAN
ROASTS

ONE PAN ROASTS

**EASY, DELICIOUS MEALS
FOR EVERY NIGHT OF THE WEEK**

Molly Shuster

MURDOCH BOOKS
SYDNEY · LONDON

CONTENTS

23 X 33 X 6.5CM

Getting a healthy home-cooked meal on to the table at dinnertime isn't always easy. Unless you adore grocery shopping and cooking, cobbling together something after a long day's work can feel simply too exhausting. This book, however, aims to change all that. Using just one cooking pan and the versatile power of an oven, you will be able to create an easy dinner, no matter what your time frame. With only a handful of ingredients and limited hands-on cooking time, you can put together a delicious meal without too much work or hassle. This book is full of simple meals that cover a wide spectrum, from easy fresh dishes that meld together in minutes under the grill, to hearty slow-cooked braises and roasts that work away in the oven all afternoon while you get on with other things.

Gathering at the dinner table was a ritual I treasured growing up; not just because food (read: eating) has always been a priority of mine, but because this was a chance to sit, reflect on the day and spend time with my family. Breaking bread with loved ones is still one of my favourite ways to gather and share news and thoughts. I hope these recipes will encourage you to share a meal with the ones you love, happily and frequently.

KITCHEN EQUIPMENT

There are just three basic tins and trays we used in creating the recipes for this book: a large 45 x 36cm baking tray for roasting and grilling; a large, deep 40 x 30cm roasting tin for roasts and braises; a smaller 23 x 33 x 6.5cm baking tin for roasting and braising. Always have foil on hand when you are roasting or grilling, to cover food if it needs protection from overbrowning or drying out.

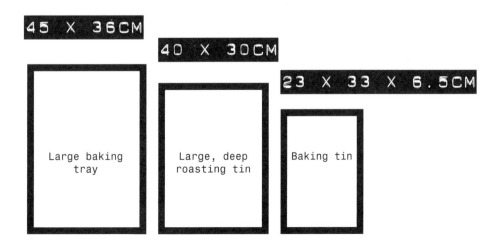

45 X 36CM — Large baking tray

40 X 30CM — Large, deep roasting tin

23 X 33 X 6.5CM — Baking tin

CREATING YOUR ONE-PAN MEAL

1 TECHNIQUE

Choose a cooking technique that will help you get the best from your main ingredient. Whether you are roasting, braising or grilling will determine the cooking time, other ingredients and method best suited for your dish.

2 COOKING PAN

Once you have chosen your technique, you need to select the appropriate pan. For roasting, use a large roasting tin. For braising, you need a deep tin or baking tray that can hold liquid. To grill, you need a grill pan or flat baking tray.

3 MAIN INGREDIENT

The options are almost endless when it comes to main ingredients suited to the oven. You might choose a meat, legume or hearty vegetable as the focal point of your one-pan roast, depending on what is in your pantry or in season. This might be chicken, beef, fish, prawns, cooked or canned beans, or firm vegetables such as cauliflower, carrots or Brussels sprouts.

4 COOKING LIQUID

When roasting or braising, you often need to add a liquid to allow the ingredients to cook through without drying out. This could be olive oil or butter, stock, wine or another water-based ingredient such as tinned chopped tomatoes.

5 AROMATICS

Aromatics such as garlic, French shallots or onions will give depth and flavour to a dish. Pick a couple to add dimension to your recipe.

6 EAT YOUR FIVE-A-DAY

Load up your meal with plenty of additional vegetables to add flavour, texture and nutrients. Choose quick-cooking vegetables such as asparagus or green beans if you are grilling, and heartier firmer vegetables such as fennel, carrots or parsnips for longer roasting and braising.

7 HERBS & SPICES

Fresh or dried herbs and spices are a very easy way to add robust flavour and character to a dish. Cook with a mix of heady spices, or add chopped bright fresh herbs just before serving, or use a combination of the two.

8 TIMING

Be sure to pay close attention to cooking time: it is essential for a delicious, well-cooked meal, whether a dish is briefly flashed under the grill for crispness or charring, or slow-roasted into tenderness. Oven and grill temperatures can vary greatly, so it is useful to have a good understanding of your own.

9 FINISHING TOUCHES

Double-check your seasoning before serving and top your dish with delicate finishing elements, such as chopped herbs, lemon zest or flaky sea salt.

10 FOR A CROWD

Pick an accompanying sauce to add another element to your meal – bright chimichurri or garlic aïoli will elevate a grill or roast to something more exciting. Adding a couple of side dishes to your roast will make it go further: polenta, farro or silky mashed potatoes will help you feed a crowd.

SAUCES

GARLIC AÏOLI

SERVES 4

2 garlic cloves, pressed through a
  garlic press or mashed to a paste
2 teaspoons lemon juice
1 egg yolk
50ml grapeseed or rapeseed oil
50ml olive oil
salt and freshly ground black pepper

Whisk garlic, lemon juice and
egg yolk in a bowl. In a very
slow, steady stream slowly
whisk in oils until emulsified
and thickened. Season to taste.
Serve at room temperature or
chilled with Roasted Salmon &
Baby Potatoes (page 68), Baked
Fish & Chips (page 72), White
Vegetable Tray (page 102) or
Grilled Squid (page 142).

LEMON CAPER SAUCE

SERVES 4

5 tablespoons olive oil
1 French shallot, finely diced
1 garlic clove, very finely chopped
1–2 anchovies, very finely chopped
50ml fresh squeezed lemon juice
2 tablespoons capers, chopped
freshly ground black pepper

Heat 3 tablespoons oil in a
pan over medium heat and sauté
shallot and garlic until
translucent but not brown.
Add anchovies and stir for
1 minute. Add lemon juice and
capers and cook for 2–3 minutes
until slightly reduced. Stir
in remaining oil. Season with
pepper. Serve warm with Roasted
Salmon & Baby Potatoes (page
68) or White Vegetable Tray
(page 102).

CHIMICHURRI SAUCE

SERVES 6–8

35g parsley, very finely chopped
35g coriander, very finely chopped
1 French shallot, finely diced
2 garlic cloves, very finely chopped
juice of ½ lemon
2 tablespoons red wine vinegar
pinch of chilli flakes (optional)
125ml olive oil
salt and freshly ground black pepper

Mix herbs with shallot, garlic, lemon juice, vinegar and chilli. Whisk in olive oil and season. Leave for 30 minutes to let flavours combine. Store in refrigerator in a sealed jar for up to 2–3 days. Serve at room temperature with Roasted Salmon & Baby Potatoes (page 68), Roasted Lemon Trout (page 76) or White Vegetable Tray (page 102).

WARM MUSTARD SAUCE

SERVES 4–6

2 tablespoons olive oil
2 French shallots, finely chopped
50ml dry white wine
1½ tablespoons Dijon mustard
1 tablespoon wholegrain mustard
75ml thick (double) cream
sea salt and freshly ground
 black pepper

Heat oil in small saucepan over medium heat. Add shallots and cook, stirring occasionally, until soft and translucent but not brown. Add wine and cook for 3 minutes until mostly reduced. Add mustards and cream and cook for 2 minutes until slightly thickened. Season to taste. Serve warm with Roasted Salmon & Baby Potatoes (page 68), Peppercorn Côte de Boeuf (page 38) or White Vegetable Tray (page 102).

ONE
PAN
ROASTS

POULTRY
& MEAT

PANCETTA CHICKEN

SERVES 2

4 bone-in chicken thighs with skin (about 650g total)
325g kipfler potatoes, scrubbed, unpeeled and halved
  lengthways
100g slab pancetta, cut into 5mm thick slices
4 French shallots, halved if large
1 rosemary sprig, finely chopped
2 teaspoons olive oil
salt and freshly ground black pepper

Preheat oven to 200°C/400°F/Gas 6. Toss all
ingredients together. Keep chicken thighs to
one side and spread remaining ingredients on
a baking tray in a single layer. Season and
roast for 15 minutes. Season chicken thighs,
add to baking tray and roast for 25 minutes,
or until chicken is cooked through and
vegetables are golden and tender.

HERBES DE PROVENCE CHICKEN

SERVES 4

4 carrots, cut into short lengths, halved
3 parsnips, cut into short lengths, halved
2 red onions, cut into fat wedges
3 tablespoons olive oil
1 chicken (about 1.8kg)
1 tablespoon herbes de Provence
sea salt and freshly ground black pepper

Preheat oven to 200°C/400°F/Gas 6. In a roasting tin, toss vegetables with half the oil. Push vegetables to edge of tin, place chicken in centre and drizzle with remaining oil. Sprinkle with herbes de Provence and season. Bake for about 1 hour 15 minutes until chicken is cooked through and vegetables are tender. Serve with Silky Mashed Potatoes (page 150), Cauliflower Purée (page 151) or Warm Quinoa Salad (page 156).

MOROCCAN CHICKEN

SERVES 4

1 chicken, quartered
1 onion, cut into 1cm thick slices
2 teaspoons ground cumin
2 teaspoons ground coriander
2 tablespoons olive oil
salt and freshly ground black pepper
100g pitted green olives, chopped
rind of 1 preserved lemon, finely chopped (you don't
  need the flesh of the lemon)

Preheat oven to 190°C/375°F/Gas 5. Toss
chicken, onion, spices and oil together on a
baking tray. Spread out in a single layer and
season. Bake for 35 minutes until chicken is
golden and cooked through. Meanwhile, mix
together olives and lemon rind and spoon over
chicken, before serving with Middle Eastern
Couscous (page 155), Warm Quinoa Salad (page
156) or Herbed Farro (page 157).

CHICKEN PUTTANESCA

SERVES 2

2 x 400g cans chopped tomatoes
65g Kalamata olives, roughly chopped
3 garlic cloves, finely chopped
2 tablespoons drained capers
½ onion, chopped
50ml olive oil
sea salt and freshly ground black pepper
450g boneless, skinless chicken breasts,
  cut into 2.5cm strips
85g baby spinach

Preheat oven to 180°C/350°F/Gas 4. Mix
tomatoes, olives, garlic, capers, onion and
oil in a roasting tin and season. Roast for
35 minutes. Stir in chicken and roast for
10 minutes, or until chicken is just cooked
through. Stir in spinach and cook for
2–3 minutes until wilted. Check seasoning.

CHICKEN SATAY

SERVES 2

75ml soy sauce
2 tablespoons toasted sesame oil
4 spring onions, sliced
2 garlic cloves, finely chopped
1 tablespoon grated fresh ginger
450g boneless, skinless chicken breasts,
  cut into 2.5cm strips
4 skewers (soaked in water for 30 minutes if wooden)
600g baby bok choy or pak choi (about 4–6 small heads),
  halved lengthways

Whisk together the soy sauce, sesame oil,
spring onions, garlic and ginger. Pour about
one-third of dressing into a small bowl and
keep on one side. Marinate chicken in
remaining dressing, covered, at room
temperature, for 30 minutes. Preheat oven to
180°C/350°F/Gas 4. Thread chicken evenly onto
4 skewers. Place on a baking tray, arrange bok
choy alongside and drizzle reserved dressing
over bok choy. Bake for about 12–15 minutes
until chicken is cooked through and bok choy
tender. Grill briefly if you like charring.

GRILLED DUCK WITH APPLES & ONIONS

SERVES 2

350g pink lady apples
350g cippolini or pearl onions, peeled
2 teaspoons olive oil
sea salt and freshly ground black pepper
2 boneless duck breasts, skin scored

Preheat oven to 200°C/400°F/Gas 6. Toss apples and onions with oil and season. Scatter on a baking tray and roast for 20 minutes. Turn the onions, then roast for another 10 minutes until apples and onions are tender. Transfer to a plate and cover to keep warm. Position rack 16cm from grill and preheat grill. Generously season duck and grill for about 5 minutes until fat has crisped and duck is medium-rare. Watch out for spitting fat. Bake in 180°C/350°F/Gas 4 oven for 3–5 minutes for well-cooked duck. Serve duck with apples and onions.

SAUSAGES WITH RED ONION & PARSNIPS

SERVES 2

2 large spicy sausages
3 parsnips, cut into short lengths, halved lengthways
2 red onions, cut into fat wedges
2 tablespoons olive oil
sea salt and freshly ground black pepper

Preheat oven to 200°C/400°F/Gas 6. Toss all ingredients on a baking tray and season. Roast for 20 minutes. Flip sausages and vegetables and roast for another 15–20 minutes until sausages are browned and vegetables are tender and golden.

CHORIZO & BEANS

SERVES 4

630g cooked white beans (300g dried)
180g dried chorizo, cut into 1cm pieces
500g tomatoes (about 3 medium), chopped
475ml chicken stock
1 onion, finely chopped
2 garlic cloves, chopped
2 thyme sprigs
salt and freshly ground black pepper
olive oil, for drizzling (optional)

Preheat oven to 180°C/350°F/Gas 4. Stir
together all ingredients in a small roasting
tin. Cover with foil and bake for 1 hour
45 minutes. Uncover and bake for 30 minutes
until stewed and thickened. Season to taste.
Drizzle with olive oil, to serve.

WINE-BRAISED OXTAIL

SERVES 4

2kg oxtail
sea salt and freshly ground black pepper
550ml dry red wine
400g carrots, cut into short pieces, halved
400g can chopped tomatoes
1 onion, chopped
few rosemary sprigs, leaves chopped
few thyme sprigs, leaves chopped

Position rack about 12cm from grill and
preheat grill. Place oxtail in small roasting
tin, season and grill for 8–10 minutes until
well browned on both sides. Preheat oven to
160°C/325°F/Gas 3. Add remaining ingredients
to roasting tin and stir together. Cover with
foil and bake for 3–4 hours or until meat is
tender and falling off bone. Using a fork,
shred meat off bones and check seasoning.
If not serving immediately, cool to room
temperature, then chill, ideally overnight.
Spoon hardened fat off top and discard.
Reheat before serving with Silky Mashed
Potatoes (page 150), Creamy Polenta (page 152)
or Classic Risotto (page 153).

SOY-MARINATED STEAK

SERVES 2

75ml soy sauce
2 tablespoons fish sauce
2 tablespoons toasted sesame oil
5 spring onions, sliced
2 garlic cloves, finely chopped
1 small skirt steak (about 500g), cut in half
400g Chinese broccoli or regular broccoli, stems
  trimmed, cut into 1.5cm thick slices

Whisk together soy sauce, fish sauce, sesame
oil, spring onions and garlic. Keep one-third
of dressing in a bowl to one side. Marinate
steak in remaining dressing, covered, at room
temperature for 30 minutes. Position rack
about 12cm from grill and preheat grill. Place
steak and broccoli on a baking tray and
drizzle with reserved dressing. Grill for
6 minutes or until steak and broccoli are
slightly charred and steak is medium done. Let
steak rest for a few minutes before slicing.

BEEF FILLETS WITH WILD MUSHROOMS

SERVES 2

2 beef tenderloin steaks (about 540g total), 6cm thick
225g mixed wild mushrooms, torn into clusters
3 French shallots, thinly sliced
2 thyme sprigs, leaves picked
2 tablespoons olive oil
sea salt and freshly ground black pepper
1 handful of chives, finely chopped

Preheat oven to 220°C/425°F/Gas 7. Place
steaks in centre of baking tray. Toss
mushrooms, shallots and thyme with oil.
Scatter around steaks and season. Roast for
15—20 minutes for medium done meat. Sprinkle
mushrooms with chives. Let steaks rest for
5 minutes before serving with Silky Mashed
Potatoes (page 150), Creamy Polenta (page 152)
or Classic Risotto (page 153).

BRAISED BEEF SHORT RIBS WITH BEANS

SERVES 4

4 bone-in beef short ribs (about 800g)
2 x 400g cans chopped tomatoes
5 carrots, cut into short lengths, halved lengthways
1 onion, sliced
4 garlic cloves, chopped
1 rosemary sprig, leaves finely chopped
325g cooked white beans (140g dried)
salt and freshly ground black pepper

Position rack about 12cm from grill and
preheat grill. Place short ribs in a roasting
tin and grill for 8–10 minutes until well
browned on both sides. Preheat oven to
160°C/325°F/Gas 3. Add tomatoes, carrots,
onion, garlic and rosemary, cover with foil
and cook for 3 hours. Stir in beans, cover and
cook for another 30 minutes. Using a fork,
shred meat away from bones. Season to taste.

PEPPERCORN CÔTE DE BOEUF

SERVES 2

1 x 5–7cm thick, bone-in côte de boeuf (about 700–900g),
  left at room temperature for 1–2 hours before cooking
2 tablespoons black peppercorns, crushed
sea salt and freshly ground black pepper
1 bunch of broccolini, trimmed
2 teaspoons olive oil

Position rack about 12cm from grill and
preheat grill. Rub beef on all sides with
crushed peppercorns and season generously with
salt. Place on a baking tray. Grill for
5 minutes. Turn steak and add broccolini.
Drizzle broccolini with oil and season. Grill
for another 5 minutes, then remove. Turn off
grill and preheat oven to 180°C/350°F/Gas 4.
Transfer broccolini to a plate and cover
to keep warm. Roast steak for 10–12 minutes
for medium-rare. Leave for 5 minutes before
slicing. Serve with Silky Mashed Potatoes
(page 150), Wild Rice Pilaf (page 154) or
Herbed Farro (page 157).

GRILLED PORK CHOPS

SERVES 2

2 bone-in pork chops, bones French-trimmed
1 teaspoon fennel seeds, crushed
1 teaspoon coriander seeds, crushed
1 teaspoon cumin seeds, crushed
leaves picked from a few thyme sprigs
1 small bunch of asparagus (about 400g), trimmed
1 tablespoon olive oil
sea salt and freshly ground black pepper

Position rack about 12cm from grill and preheat grill. Place pork on a baking tray. Mix spices and thyme together and rub all over pork. Place asparagus on baking tray, drizzle oil over pork and asparagus and season generously. Toss asparagus and spread out in a single layer. Grill for 5–10 minutes, or until pork is just cooked through and asparagus is tender and golden in spots.

SIMPLE PORK TENDERLOIN ROAST

SERVES 2

1 pork tenderloin roast (about 450g)
1 rosemary sprig, leaves finely chopped
2 tablespoons wholegrain mustard
2 tablespoons plus 1 teaspoon olive oil
sea salt and freshly ground black pepper
225g Brussels sprouts, halved if large
4 small French shallots, halved lengthways

Preheat oven to 200°C/400°F/Gas 6. Rub pork
with rosemary and mustard. Place on a baking
tray, drizzle with 1 teaspoon oil and season.
Toss Brussels sprouts and shallots with
remaining oil, then scatter around pork.
Bake for 30–35 minutes, or until pork is
cooked through. Serve with Cauliflower Purée
(page 151), Wild Rice Pilaf (page 154) or
Warm Quinoa Salad (page 156).

PORK SHOULDER ROAST

SERVES 6

1 bone-in pork shoulder, about 3–3.5kg, left at room
  temperature for 1–2 hours before cooking
salt and freshly ground black pepper
1 bunch of rosemary, half leaves very finely chopped,
  half of stems reserved
1 bunch of sage, half leaves very finely chopped
650g parsnips, cut into short lengths, halved
  lengthways if large
2 onions, cut into fat wedges
500g pink lady apples (about 8)

Preheat oven to 220°C/425°F/Gas 7. Using a
sharp knife, score a cross-hatch pattern into
the pork skin, leaving a thin layer of fat and
being careful not to cut down to the flesh.
Season pork well on all sides and into the
score marks. Rub all over with chopped herbs.
Place skin-side up in a large roasting tin and
roast for 30 minutes. Lower heat to
160°C/325°F/Gas 3. Cover tightly with foil and
roast for 4 hours. Uncover, add parsnips,
onions, apples and reserved herbs and toss
with fat in the tin. Roast, uncovered, for
about 1 hour 15 minutes until pork is tender.
Rest meat for 10 minutes before serving.

BRAISED LAMB SHANKS

SERVES 4

3 lamb shanks (about 1kg total)
sea salt and freshly ground black pepper
2 x 400g cans chopped tomatoes
250g carrots, cut into short lengths, halved lengthways
1 onion, sliced
3 garlic cloves, chopped
2 rosemary sprigs, leaves chopped
100g Israeli couscous, uncooked

Position rack about 12cm from grill and preheat
grill. Place lamb in a roasting tin and season.
Grill for 8—10 minutes until well browned on both
sides. Add 400ml water and remaining ingredients
except couscous, and stir to combine. Cover with
foil. Preheat oven to 160°C/325°F/Gas 3 and cook
for 2½—3 hours until tender, turning meat once.
Stir in couscous, cover and return to oven for
another 30 minutes until couscous is cooked and
meat is tender and falling off bones. Shred meat,
discarding bones, and season to taste.

SLOW-COOKED LAMB SHOULDER

SERVES 4–6

1 bone-in lamb shoulder, about 3kg, left at room
temperature for 1–2 hours before cooking
2 tablespoons olive oil
juice of 1 lemon
2 tablespoons sea salt
2 tablespoons fennel seeds, crushed
1 tablespoon coriander seeds, crushed
1 teaspoon chilli flakes
freshly ground black pepper
2 red onions, cut into wedges
2 fennel bulbs, quartered, cored and cut into wedges

Preheat oven to 160°C/325°F/Gas 3. Place lamb
in a large roasting tin and drizzle with oil
and lemon juice. Mix salt and spices together
and rub all over roast. Season with pepper.
Cover with foil and roast for 3 hours. Check
occasionally, adding 50ml water if dry. After
3 hours, add onion and fennel. Cover and cook
for 1½–2 hours until vegetables are cooked and
meat is tender. Remove from oven and preheat
grill. Place rack low enough so top of roast
is about 15cm from grill. Grill for about
5 minutes, checking frequently, until browned.
Tent loosely with foil and rest for 10 minutes
before serving with Silky Mashed Potatoes
(page 150), Wild Rice Pilaf (page 154) or
Herbed Farro (page 157).

ONE
PAN
ROASTS

SEAFOOD

PRAWN PANZANELLA

SERVES 2

200g day-old crusty bread, torn into bite-sized pieces
12 prawns, peeled and deveined
50ml plus 1 teaspoon olive oil
sea salt and freshly ground black pepper
250g cherry tomatoes, halved
3 tablespoons balsamic vinegar
1 garlic clove, very finely chopped
1 small bunch of basil, leaves roughly chopped
1 small bunch of parsley, leaves chopped

Preheat oven to 180°C/350°F/Gas 4. Spread torn
bread in a single layer on a baking tray. Bake
for 10 minutes. Toss bread and push to one
side of tray. Toss prawns with 1 teaspoon oil
and arrange on baking tray. Season and bake
for 5–7 minutes until prawns are cooked
through and bread is toasted. Add remaining
ingredients, toss well and season to taste.

HARISSA PRAWNS & EGGPLANT

SERVES 2

1 tablespoon harissa
3 tablespoons olive oil
1 eggplant (aubergine), cut into 1cm thick slices, halved if large
12 prawns, peeled and deveined
2 spring onions, sliced

Preheat oven to 200°C/400°F/Gas 6. Mix harissa and oil together and toss eggplant with two-thirds of harissa mixture. Spread eggplant on a baking tray and roast for 20 minutes. Mix prawns and spring onions with remaining harissa mixture. Toss eggplant and push to one side of the tray to make space for prawns. Spread out prawns in a single layer and roast for about 5 minutes or until just cooked through and eggplant is tender.

GRILLED SCALLOPS WITH SUMMER VEGETABLES

SERVES 2

300g grape or cherry tomatoes, halved
2 baby pumpkins, cut into 5mm thick slices
4 spring onions, chopped
2 tablespoons olive oil
450g sea scallops
sea salt and freshly ground black pepper
1 handful of basil leaves, torn

Position rack about 12cm from grill and
preheat grill. Toss tomatoes, pumpkin and
spring onions with 1 tablespoon oil. Scatter
vegetables over one side of a baking tray. Add
scallops to the tray, drizzle with remaining
oil and season. Grill for about 10 minutes
until scallops are just cooked and vegetables
tender. Garnish with basil.

BURST CHERRY TOMATOES WITH CLAMS

SERVES 2

850g cherry or grape tomatoes
2 garlic cloves, thinly sliced
150ml dry vermouth or dry white wine
3 tablespoons olive oil
sea salt and freshly ground black pepper
700g small clams, scrubbed and rinsed
1 handful of basil leaves, torn

Preheat oven to 180°C/350°F/Gas 4. Place
tomatoes, garlic, vermouth and oil in a small
roasting tin. Season. Roast for 40 minutes, or
until tomatoes have shrivelled and begun to
burst. Stir in clams and cover tightly with
foil. Bake for 5–8 minutes until clams open
(discard any that remain closed). Garnish
with basil.

CREAMY MUSSELS

SERVES 2–4

1 leek, pale part only, halved and cut 5mm thick
2 garlic cloves, sliced
175ml white wine
175ml thick (double) cream
900g mussels, scrubbed and rinsed

Preheat oven to 180°C/350°F/Gas 4. Put leek, garlic, wine and cream in a small roasting tin. Cover with foil and bake for 15 minutes. Add mussels and stir well. Cover tightly and bake for 8–10 minutes, just until the mussels open. Discard any mussels that remain closed.

SEARED TUNA & MUSHROOMS

SERVES 2

225g shiitake mushrooms, trimmed, halved if large
6 spring onions
2 tablespoons low-sodium soy sauce
2 teaspoons toasted sesame oil
1 large thick tuna steak (about 375g)

Preheat oven to 220°C/425°F/Gas 7. Toss
mushrooms and spring onions with soy sauce and
1 teaspoon sesame oil. Spread in an even layer
on a baking tray and bake for 5 minutes.
Remove tray and preheat grill. Drizzle tuna
with remaining oil and place on baking tray.
Grill for about 2 minutes, or until spring
onions are lightly charred and tuna is cooked
outside but pink inside. Slice tuna and serve
warm with mushrooms and spring onions. Drizzle
with extra soy sauce, if you like.

PROSCIUTTO-WRAPPED MONKFISH

SERVES 2

1 monkfish fillet (about 400g)
a few thyme sprigs
50g thinly sliced prosciutto
180g green beans, trimmed
2 teaspoons olive oil
sea salt and freshly ground black pepper

Preheat oven to 200°C/400°F/Gas 6. Pat monkfish dry, sprinkle with thyme leaves and wrap in prosciutto to fully encase the fish. Place on a baking tray. Toss green beans with oil, spread out on the tray and season. Bake for about 12—15 minutes until monkfish is cooked through and prosciutto is crisp. Serve with Silky Mashed Potatoes (page 150), Classic Risotto (page 153) or Warm Quinoa Salad (page 156).

HARISSA SALMON

SERVES 2

350g baby potatoes, cut into 5mm thick slices
4 teaspoons olive oil
sea salt and freshly ground black pepper
180g green beans, trimmed
2 thick salmon fillets (about 400g total)
2 teaspoons harissa paste
85g pitted green olives, chopped

Preheat oven to 200°C/400°F/Gas 6. Toss
potatoes with half the oil, season and spread
out on a baking tray. Roast for 15 minutes.
Toss potatoes, then push them to one side of
tray. Toss green beans with remaining oil and
place on tray. Rub salmon with harissa, then
add to tray. Bake for 12–15 minutes, or until
salmon is cooked through to your taste.
Scatter with olives.

ROASTED SALMON & BABY POTATOES

SERVES 2

350g baby potatoes, halved lengthways
2 teaspoons olive oil
salt and freshly ground black pepper
2 thick salmon fillets (about 400g total)

Preheat oven to 200°C/400°F/Gas 6. Toss
potatoes with oil, season and spread out on
a baking tray. Roast for 20 minutes. Toss
potatoes and push to one side of tray, to make
enough room for the fish. Add salmon and roast
for 10–15 minutes until cooked through.
Serve with Chimichurri Sauce, Warm Mustard
Sauce, Lemon Caper Sauce or Garlic Aïoli
(pages 10–11).

BRAISED COD WITH TOMATOES & OLIVES

SERVES 2

700g tomatoes, chopped into large bite-sized pieces
200g baby potatoes, cut into thin slices (about
  5mm thick)
50g Kalamata olives, roughly chopped
2 garlic cloves, chopped
2 oregano sprigs, leaves picked
2 tablespoons olive oil
sea salt and freshly ground black pepper
450g cod loin, cut into large bite-sized pieces
few parsley sprigs, chopped

Preheat oven to 180°C/350°F/Gas 4. Place
tomatoes, potatoes, olives, garlic and oregano
in a small roasting tin. Drizzle with oil,
season and stir together. Cover loosely with
foil and bake for 1 hour. Stir in cod and
parsley. Cover again and bake for 10 minutes,
or until potatoes are tender and fish is just
cooked through. Check seasoning.

BAKED FISH & CHIPS

SERVES 2

300g baby potatoes, very thinly sliced
1 rosemary sprig, finely chopped
3 tablespoons olive oil, plus extra for drizzling
60g plain flour
60g dried breadcrumbs
sea salt and freshly ground black pepper
450g cod loin, cut into 2.5cm thick strips
1 egg, lightly beaten with 1 tablespoon water
lemon wedges, to serve

Preheat oven to 200°C/400°F/Gas 6. Toss
potatoes with rosemary and oil. Season
generously and spread out on a baking tray.
Roast for 15 minutes. Meanwhile, spread flour
and breadcrumbs on separate plates. Season
breadcrumbs with salt. Dredge fish strips in
flour, one by one, shaking off excess. Dip into
beaten egg, then dredge with breadcrumbs. Toss
potatoes and push to side of tray to make room
for fish. Add fish and drizzle lightly with oil.
Bake for 12—15 minutes until fish is cooked
through and potatoes are crisp golden brown.
Serve with lemon wedges and sea salt.

ASIAN STEAMED SOLE

SERVES 2

2 sole fillets (or 4 if small)
1 small bunch tender spinach (or a few handfuls
   baby spinach)
200g enoki mushrooms, trimmed
1 tablespoon soy sauce
1 teaspoon toasted sesame oil
1 teaspoon toasted sesame seeds

Preheat oven to 180°C/350°F/Gas 4. Place sole
fillets in a single, snug layer on one side of
a baking tray. Spread spinach on other side
of tray and scatter mushrooms on top. Whisk
together soy sauce, oil and sesame seeds and
drizzle over whole tray. Cover tightly with
foil. Bake for 10–12 minutes, or until fish is
just cooked through and spinach has wilted.

ROASTED LEMON TROUT

SERVES 2

2 whole trout (about 900g total), cleaned and gutted
2 small lemons, cut into thin slices
1 handful of thyme
2 tablespoons olive oil
sea salt and freshly ground black pepper

Preheat oven to 220°C/425°F/Gas 7. Fill cavity
of each trout with lemon slices and thyme. Tie
trout tightly with string every 5cm and rub
fish all over with oil. Place on a baking tray
and season well. Roast for 15–20 minutes, or
until fish is just cooked through. Serve with
Chimichurri, Lemon Caper Sauce or Garlic Aioli
(pages 10–11).

ONE
PAN
ROASTS

VEGETABLES

STUFFED PUMPKINS

SERVES 4

2 baby pumpkins
3 large French shallots, finely chopped
200g day-old crusty bread, torn into 3–5cm pieces
125g unsalted butter, melted
80g dried cranberries
2 rosemary sprigs, leaves chopped
250ml chicken stock
salt and freshly ground black pepper
4 tablespoons extra virgin olive oil

Preheat oven to 180°C/350°F/Gas 4. Cut
pumpkins in half and scoop out seeds. Mix
together shallots, bread, butter, cranberries,
rosemary and chicken stock and season well.
Divide evenly between pumpkin halves. Place on
a baking tray and drizzle with oil. Tent with
foil and bake for 1 hour 30 minutes. Uncover
and bake for another 20 minutes until pumpkin
is tender and stuffing is golden and crisp.

STUFFED PORTOBELLO MUSHROOMS

SERVES 4

4 Portobello mushrooms, stems removed
4 tablespoons olive oil
sea salt and freshly ground black pepper
250g cooked pearl barley (125g uncooked)
75g feta cheese, crumbled
35g toasted walnuts, chopped
2 tablespoons chopped parsley
2 tablespoons chopped mint
80g pomegranate seeds

Preheat oven to 180°C/350°F/Gas 4. Place
mushrooms, skin-side-down, on a baking tray,
drizzle with 2 tablespoons oil and season to
taste. Bake for 15 minutes. Meanwhile, mix
together barley, feta, walnuts, parsley and
1 tablespoon mint. Stuff mushrooms with
filling, drizzle with remaining oil and bake
for another 15 minutes. Sprinkle with
pomegranate seeds and remaining mint to serve.

TRAY BEANS

SERVES 4

450g dried cannellini beans, soaked overnight
750ml chicken stock
100g Parmesan rind
3 bay leaves
2 garlic cloves, peeled
1 rosemary sprig
2 tablespoons olive oil, plus extra for drizzling
sea salt and freshly ground black pepper

Preheat oven to 160°C/325°F/Gas 3. Drain the
beans and combine with the other ingredients
in a 23 x 33 x 6.5cm baking tin. Cover with
foil and bake for about 1 hour 30 minutes
until beans are tender and liquid has
thickened. Remove Parmesan rind and serve,
drizzled with a little extra olive oil.

WHOLE ROASTED CAULIFLOWER

SERVES 4–6

1 cauliflower, cored, leaves trimmed
300ml dry white wine
5 strips zest and juice of 1 lemon
few thyme sprigs
3 tablespoons olive oil
130g green olives, chopped
75g toasted hazelnuts, chopped

Preheat oven to 190°C/375°F/Gas 5. Place cauliflower in a 23 x 33 x 6.5cm baking tin. Add wine, lemon zest and juice and thyme. Drizzle cauliflower with oil. Cover with foil and bake 45 minutes–1 hour until almost tender. Add a little water if pan is dry. Uncover and bake for another 25 minutes until golden. Meanwhile, combine olives and hazelnuts. Lift out cauliflower onto a serving dish and serve with olive mixture and perhaps Wild Rice Pilaf (page 154), Warm Quinoa Salad (page 156) or Herbed Farro (page 157).

BAKED HALLOUMI

SERVES 2–4

1 bunch Swiss chard (about 330g), roughly chopped
3 vine tomatoes, about 450g, cut into 5mm slices
3 spring onions, sliced
1 garlic clove, very finely chopped
50ml olive oil
230g halloumi cheese, cut into 5mm thick slices
sea salt and freshly ground black pepper

Preheat oven to 200°C/400°F/Gas 6. On a baking
tray, toss Swiss chard, tomatoes, spring
onions and garlic with all but 2 teaspoons of
oil. Spread out in an even layer on the tray.
Scatter with halloumi and drizzle halloumi
with remaining oil. Season well. Bake for
15 minutes or until vegetables are tender and
just beginning to release their juices. Remove
from oven and preheat grill. Grill tray for
1–2 minutes until cheese is golden. Keep an
eye on tray: if Swiss chard begins to burn,
loosely tent area with a small piece of foil.
Serve with Wild Rice Pilaf (page 154) or
Herbed Farro (page 157).

BLUE CHEESE ENDIVE

SERVES 4

4 endive, halved lengthways
1 tablespoon olive oil
freshly ground black pepper
80g blue cheese, crumbled
40g walnuts, chopped

Preheat oven to 200°C/400°F/Gas 6. Place
endive, cut-side-up, on a baking tray,
drizzle with olive oil and season with pepper.
Roast for 20 minutes. Scatter evenly with blue
cheese and walnuts. Roast for 5—10 minutes
until endive is tender and cheese has melted.

ROASTED RADICCHIO WITH BALSAMIC & PARMESAN

SERVES 2

4 tablespoons balsamic vinegar
2 heads radicchio, quartered and cores trimmed
2 tablespoons olive oil
sea salt and freshly ground black pepper
4 tablespoons grated Parmesan cheese

Preheat oven to 200°C/400°F/Gas 6. Put vinegar in a small pan and simmer over medium heat until syrupy and reduced by half. Place radicchio on a baking tray and drizzle with oil. Season. Roast for about 10 minutes until slightly tender and leaves are lightly charred. Grill briefly, for extra crispiness, if desired. Drizzle with balsamic vinegar and sprinkle with Parmesan cheese. Serve with Creamy Polenta (page 152) or Classic Risotto (page 153).

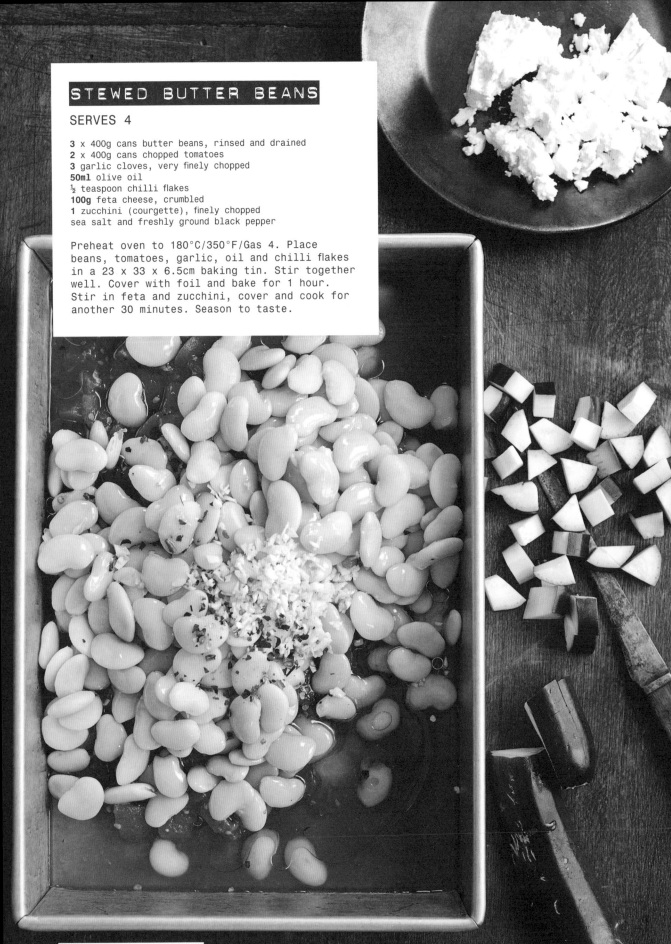

STEWED BUTTER BEANS

SERVES 4

3 x 400g cans butter beans, rinsed and drained
2 x 400g cans chopped tomatoes
3 garlic cloves, very finely chopped
50ml olive oil
½ teaspoon chilli flakes
100g feta cheese, crumbled
1 zucchini (courgette), finely chopped
sea salt and freshly ground black pepper

Preheat oven to 180°C/350°F/Gas 4. Place
beans, tomatoes, garlic, oil and chilli flakes
in a 23 x 33 x 6.5cm baking tin. Stir together
well. Cover with foil and bake for 1 hour.
Stir in feta and zucchini, cover and cook for
another 30 minutes. Season to taste.

QUINOA-STUFFED ZUCCHINI

SERVES 4

2 zucchini (courgettes)
200g cooked white quinoa (60g dried)
25g toasted pine nuts
150ml tomato pasta sauce
115g fresh mozzarella, grated
1 handful of small basil leaves

Preheat oven to 180°C/350°F/Gas 4. Scoop seeds and a little additional flesh from zucchini to make boats for filling. Combine quinoa, pine nuts, half the pasta sauce and half the mozzarella and spoon into zucchini. Top with remaining sauce and mozzarella. Bake for about 40 minutes until zucchini are cooked through and cheese is golden and melted. Top with basil leaves.

SHAKSHUKA

SERVES 4—6

750g tomatoes, chopped
1 red capsicum (pepper), chopped
1 yellow capsicum (pepper), chopped
2 garlic cloves, very finely chopped
½ teaspoon hot paprika
50ml olive oil
1 handful of parsley, chopped
sea salt and freshly ground black pepper
6 eggs

Preheat oven to 180°C/350°F/Gas 4. Mix together tomatoes, capsicum, garlic, paprika and oil in a 23 x 33 x 6.5cm baking tin. Add about half the parsley and season. Bake, uncovered, for 1 hour. Use a spoon to make 6 hollows in the sauce. Crack the eggs into the hollows and bake for 12—15 minutes until just set. Sprinkle with remaining parsley.

BALSAMIC BRUSSELS SPROUTS

SERVES 2—4

3 tablespoons balsamic vinegar
800g Brussels sprouts, trimmed, halved if large
100g slab pancetta, diced
2 tablespoons olive oil
sea salt and freshly ground black pepper

Preheat oven to 200°C/400°F/Gas 6. Put vinegar in a small pan and simmer over medium heat until syrupy and reduced by half. On a baking tray, toss Brussels sprouts and pancetta with oil and season. Spread out in an even layer on tray and roast for 20 minutes. Toss, then roast for another 10 minutes until golden and tender. Toss with syrupy balsamic vinegar.

WHITE VEGETABLE TRAY

SERVES 2—4

350g Jerusalem artichokes, scrubbed and cut into
  5mm thick slices
1 large fennel bulb, quartered, cored and cut
  into 2.5cm thick wedges
3 small endive, halved lengthways
2 leeks, light parts only, halved lengthways and cut
  into 8cm pieces
2 tablespoons olive oil
sea salt and freshly ground black pepper

Preheat oven to 220°C/425°F/Gas 7. On a baking
tray, toss vegetables with oil and season.
Spread out in an even layer. Roast for about
35—40 minutes, tossing once, until vegetables
are golden and tender. Serve with Garlic Aïoli
(page 10) or Lemon Caper Sauce (page 10) and
Creamy Polenta (page 152), Classic Risotto
(page 153) or Warm Quinoa Salad (page 156).

BABY EGGPLANT WITH BURRATA

SERVES 4

4 baby or small Japanese eggplant (aubergines)
100ml olive oil
sea salt and freshly ground black pepper
1 oregano sprig, leaves picked
1 small ball burrata cheese (about 250g)
1 handful of basil leaves, torn if large

Preheat oven to 200°C/400°F/Gas 6. Cut
eggplant, starting about 2.5cm away from stem
so they hold together, slicing in half
lengthways. Place on a baking tray and drizzle
with oil, taking care to drizzle oil on both
cut flesh and skin. Season generously and
sprinkle oregano leaves in cavity of eggplant.
Roast for 40 minutes, turning once, until
completely tender and lightly golden. Top each
with a piece of torn burrata and some basil.

CAULIFLOWER & LENTILS

SERVES 4

1 cauliflower, cut into small florets
1 onion, thinly sliced
2 tablespoons olive oil
1 teaspoon ground cumin
sea salt and freshly ground black pepper
260g cooked Puy lentils (100g dried)
2 tablespoons dried currants, plumped in
  hot water and drained
2 tablespoons toasted pine nuts

Preheat oven to 200°C/400°F/Gas 6. On a baking
tray, toss cauliflower florets, onion, oil and
cumin. Spread out in an even layer and season.
Roast for 25 minutes or until cauliflower and
onion are tender and beginning to colour. Add
lentils, currants and pine nuts and toss to
combine. Roast for about 10 minutes until
vegetables are lightly golden. Serve warm or
at room temperature.

RED VEGETABLE CURRY

SERVES 4

400ml can coconut milk
3 tablespoons red curry paste
1 onion, thinly sliced
4 carrots, cut into 5mm thick rounds on the bias
sea salt
300g broccoli, broken into small florets
1 red capsicum (pepper), chopped
80g toasted cashews

Preheat oven to 180°C/350°F/Gas 4. In a
22 x 33 x 6.5cm baking tin, stir together
coconut milk, curry paste, onion and carrots
and season with salt. Cover with foil and cook
for 20 minutes. Stir in broccoli and capsicum,
cover again and cook for 5—10 minutes until
tender. Check seasoning and sprinkle with
toasted cashews to serve.

ONE
PAN
ROASTS

DESSERTS

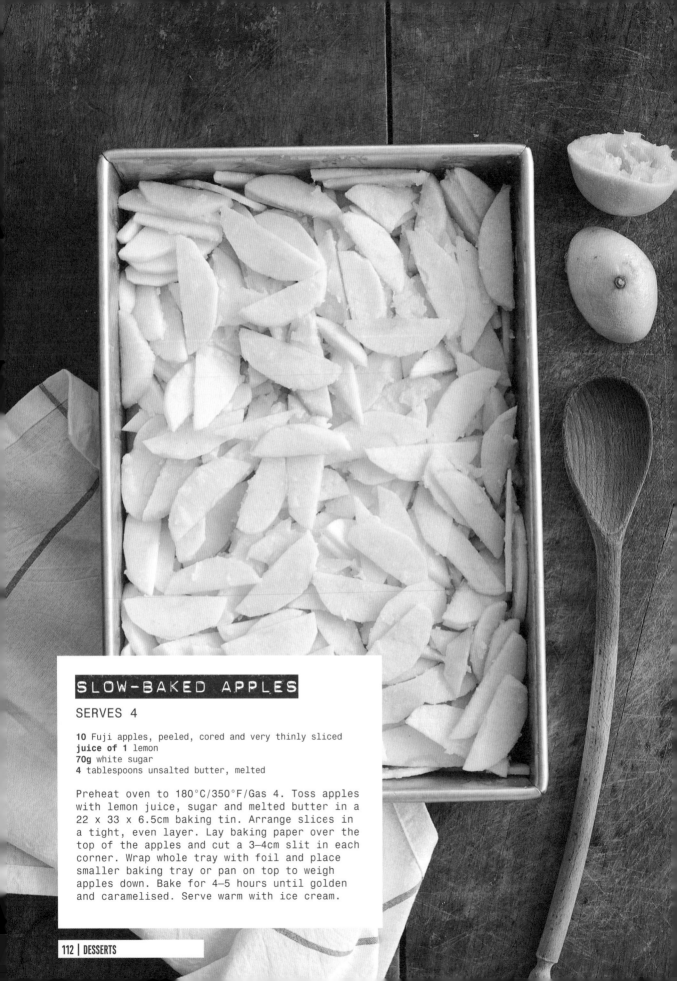

SLOW-BAKED APPLES

SERVES 4

10 Fuji apples, peeled, cored and very thinly sliced
juice of 1 lemon
70g white sugar
4 tablespoons unsalted butter, melted

Preheat oven to 180°C/350°F/Gas 4. Toss apples
with lemon juice, sugar and melted butter in a
22 x 33 x 6.5cm baking tin. Arrange slices in
a tight, even layer. Lay baking paper over the
top of the apples and cut a 3–4cm slit in each
corner. Wrap whole tray with foil and place
smaller baking tray or pan on top to weigh
apples down. Bake for 4–5 hours until golden
and caramelised. Serve warm with ice cream.

APPLE CRUMBLE

SERVES 4

4 Fuji apples
100g rolled oats
80g light brown sugar
80g walnuts, finely chopped
125g unsalted butter, melted
½ teaspoon ground cinnamon

Preheat oven to 180°C/350°F/Gas 4. Cut apples
into thirds horizontally. Using a melon
baller, scoop out core from each slice of
apple. Mix together remaining ingredients to
make crumble filling. Place bottom of each
apple on a baking tray and scatter with
filling. Place middle of each apple on top and
secure with toothpicks. Scatter with more
crumble filling. Place tops on apples and
secure with toothpicks. Sprinkle any remaining
crumble over tops of apples. Bake for about
45 minutes or until apples are tender and
filling is golden. Cool slightly. Carefully
remove toothpicks before serving warm.

MAPLE BAKED PEARS

SERVES 8

4 Williams or Red Bartlett pears
100g pecans, finely chopped
4 tablespoons unsalted butter, melted
4 tablespoons maple syrup
½ teaspoon ground cinnamon
¼ teaspoon ground cloves
pinch of salt

Preheat oven to 180°C/350°F/Gas 4. Halve pears
lengthways and use a melon baller to scoop out
cores and a little extra flesh to make room for
filling. Place on a baking tray. Mix together
remaining ingredients and spoon onto pears.
Bake for 30 minutes until fruit is tender and
filling is golden. Serve warm.

SPICE-ROASTED PINEAPPLE

SERVES 4

1 pineapple, peeled, cored and cut into 5mm thick slices
1 vanilla pod, split lengthways and seeds scraped out
50g white sugar
2 cinnamon sticks, broken
2 star anise
2 tablespoons unsalted butter, diced

Preheat oven to 180°C/350°F/Gas 4. Toss together all ingredients, except butter, on a baking tray. Dot pineapple with butter. Roast for 30–40 minutes, turn pineapple and roast for another 20–30 minutes until golden brown. Serve warm.

VANILLA-ROASTED APRICOTS

SERVES 4

1kg apricots, halved
1 vanilla pod, split in half lengthways and seeds
scraped out
4 tablespoons unsalted butter, melted
4 tablespoons light brown sugar
juice of ½ lemon
170g raspberries

Preheat oven to 180°C/350°F/Gas 4. Toss
all ingredients, except raspberries, in a
23 x 33 x 6.5cm baking tin. Bake for about
40 minutes until fruit is tender and syrupy.
Stir in raspberries and bake for another
5 minutes. Serve warm or at room temperature.

CHERRY CLAFOUTIS

SERVES 6

4 tablespoons unsalted butter, plus extra for greasing
8 large eggs, lightly beaten
250ml milk
150ml double (thick) cream
100g sugar
50g plain flour
pinch of salt
250g cherries, pitted

Preheat oven to 190°C/375°F/Gas 5 and butter a 23 x 33 x 6.5cm baking tin. Blend all ingredients, except cherries, until smooth. Discard any foam. Pour into tin and dot evenly with cherries. Bake for 35—40 minutes until just set and lightly golden. Serve warm, at room temperature or chilled.

PEACH CUSTARD TART

SERVES 6—8

1 sheet of frozen puff pastry, thawed
225ml double (thick) cream
50g sugar
2 eggs
½ teaspoon vanilla extract
600g peaches or apricots, cut into thin wedges

Preheat oven to 200°C/400°F/Gas 6. Roll out
pastry to 25 x 30cm. Place pastry on a baking
tray. Fold edges of pastry to create 2.5cm thick
borders on each side. Prick centre with fork.
Cover with foil and weigh down with baking beans,
uncooked rice or pie weights. Leave folded wedges
unweighted. Bake for about 15 minutes until
lightly golden. Remove weights and foil and bake
for another 5 minutes. Cool slightly. Reduce
heat to 180°C/350°F/Gas 4. Whisk together cream,
sugar, eggs and vanilla. Pour into baked case and
top with sliced fruit. Bake for about 40 minutes
until custard is set and fruit is tender.
Serve on the day of baking, either warm or at
room temperature.

ONE
PAN
ROASTS

SNACKS & APPETISERS

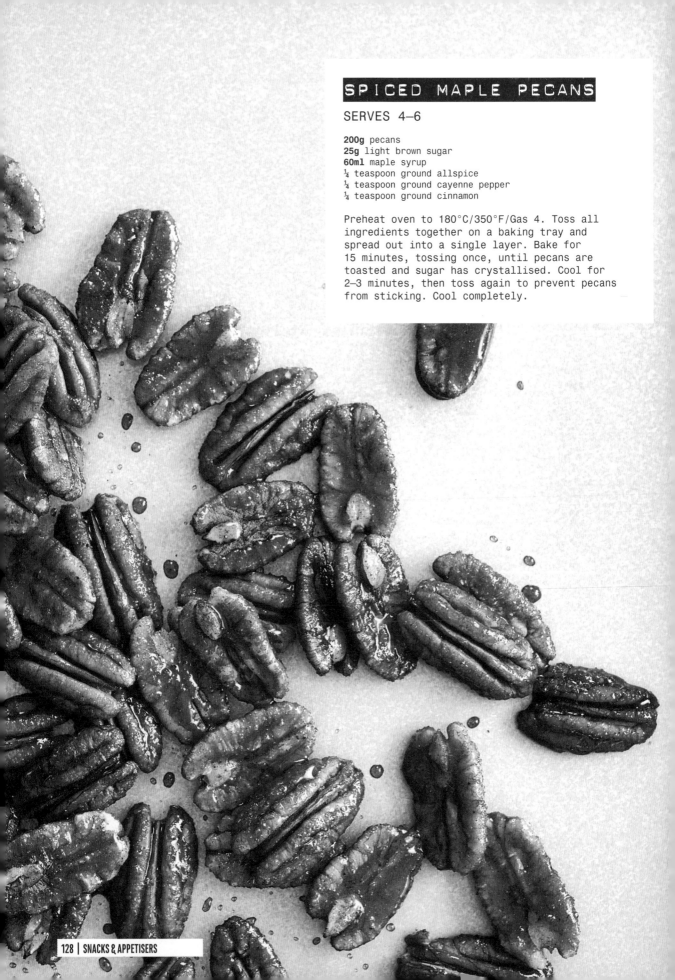

SPICED MAPLE PECANS

SERVES 4–6

200g pecans
25g light brown sugar
60ml maple syrup
¼ teaspoon ground allspice
¼ teaspoon ground cayenne pepper
¼ teaspoon ground cinnamon

Preheat oven to 180°C/350°F/Gas 4. Toss all ingredients together on a baking tray and spread out into a single layer. Bake for 15 minutes, tossing once, until pecans are toasted and sugar has crystallised. Cool for 2–3 minutes, then toss again to prevent pecans from sticking. Cool completely.

LEMON-PARMESAN ARTICHOKE HEARTS

SERVES 6

6 large, olive oil-marinated artichoke hearts with stems
2 teaspoons olive oil
2 thyme sprigs, leaves picked
grated zest and juice of ½ lemon
2½ tablespoons grated Parmesan cheese

Position oven rack about 12cm from grill and preheat grill. Halve artichokes lengthways, place cut-side-up on a baking tray and drizzle with oil. Sprinkle with thyme leaves and lemon zest. Grill for 2–3 minutes until lightly charred. Drizzle with lemon juice and sprinkle with Parmesan. Serve warm.

BABA GANOUSH

SERVES 6–8

2 eggplant (aubergines)
2 teaspoons olive oil
60g tahini
1 small handful of parsley leaves
2 garlic cloves, chopped
1½ tablespoons lemon juice
sea salt

Position oven rack about 12cm from grill and preheat grill. Place eggplant on a baking tray, rub with oil and grill for 2–4 minutes each side until well charred on all sides. Turn oven to 200°C/400°F/Gas 6 and roast for about 10 minutes until tender. Cut eggplant in half and cool to room temperature. Scoop eggplant flesh into food processor and discard skins. Add remaining ingredients and blend until smooth. Add salt to taste.

CHICKEN LIVER PATE

SERVES 4

400g chicken livers, rinsed and dried
1 small sweet onion, very thinly sliced
50g chicken fat, butter or olive oil, melted
2 hard-boiled eggs, finely chopped
3 tablespoons dried currants, left to plump in a bowl
  of hot water and drained
sea salt

Position oven rack about 12cm from grill and preheat grill. Place chicken livers on one side of a baking tray and toss onion with half the chicken fat on the other side of the tray. Grill for about 5–7 minutes until chicken livers are cooked through and onion is tender and charred in a few places. Cool slightly. Finely chop chicken livers, onion and fat (leave any blood behind). Stir in eggs, currants and remaining fat and season to taste with a little salt.

SLOW-ROASTED CHERRY TOMATO BRUSCHETTA

SERVES 6—8

550g cherry or grape tomatoes
2 tablespoons olive oil
sea salt and freshly ground black pepper
toasted baguette, to serve
fresh ricotta, to serve

Preheat oven to 160°C/325°F/Gas 3. Place
tomatoes on a baking tray and drizzle with
oil. Season. Roast for about 1 hour 15 minutes
until tomatoes are shrivelled and just
beginning to burst. Serve tomatoes warm on
toasted baguette with ricotta.

PARSNIP SOUP

SERVES 2

400g parsnips, cut into 3–5cm pieces
2 French shallots, quartered
1 tablespoon olive oil
sea salt and freshly ground black pepper
350ml chicken stock, heated
150ml milk, heated
2 tablespoons double (thick) cream, heated
fresh herbs, such as chervil, chives or tarragon, finely
  chopped, to garnish

Preheat oven to 200°C/400°F/Gas 6. Toss
parsnips and shallots with oil and season.
Spread out into an even layer on a baking
tray. Roast for 25–30 minutes until tender and
lightly golden, tossing once. Purée
vegetables, stock and milk in blender until
completely smooth. Stir in cream. Add a little
extra milk if too thick. Check seasoning.
Garnish with finely chopped fresh herbs.

NACHOS

SERVES 6

1 bag corn tortilla chips (about 450g)
150g canned black beans, rinsed and drained
150g blackened corn kernels (from 2 grilled corn cobs)
250g fresh tomato salsa
3 avocados, diced
200g grated Cheddar cheese
6 radishes, thinly sliced

Position oven rack about 12cm from grill and preheat grill. Spread chips on a baking tray. Layer with beans, corn, salsa, avocado and cheese and grill for 3–5 minutes, until cheese is melted and browned. Scatter with radishes.

GRILLED SQUID

SERVES 4–6

450g squid, cleaned, rinsed and patted dry,
  bodies cut into rounds
200ml olive oil
2 garlic cloves, thinly sliced
½ teaspoon chilli flakes
4 heaped tablespoons fresh breadcrumbs
1 lemon, cut into wedges, to serve
sea salt

Place squid, oil, garlic and chilli flakes
in a bowl and leave to marinate at room
temperature for 1 hour. Position oven rack
about 12cm from grill and preheat grill. Drain
marinade from squid and arrange squid on
baking tray. Sprinkle with breadcrumbs. Grill
squid for 2 minutes until just cooked through,
taking care not to burn the breadcrumbs. Serve
with lemon wedges and sea salt.

BRAISED BABY OCTOPUS

SERVES 2—4

8 baby octopus (about 450g total)
200g canned chickpeas, rinsed
350g tomatoes, finely chopped
3 garlic cloves, finely chopped
2 teaspoons Dijon mustard
1 oregano sprig, leaves picked
½ teaspoon paprika
50ml olive oil
sea salt and freshly ground black pepper

Preheat oven to 160°C/325°F/Gas 3. Mix
together all ingredients in a small deep
baking tin. Cover with foil and cook for about
40 minutes until octopus is tender and only
retains a slight chewiness. Season to taste.

SWEET & SPICY CHICKEN

SERVES 4–6

675g chicken wings
675g chicken drumsticks
1 tablespoon olive oil
sea salt and freshly ground black pepper
40ml Sriracha (hot chilli) sauce
40ml honey
1 tablespoon Worcestershire sauce

Preheat oven to 230°C/450°F/Gas 8. On a baking
tray, toss chicken wings and drumsticks with
oil and season generously. Spread out in a
single layer. Roast for about 25–30 minutes,
turning once, until golden and cooked through.
Meanwhile, combine Sriracha, honey and
Worcestershire sauce in a large bowl. Using
tongs, transfer cooked chicken to sauce bowl
and toss to coat. Drain fat from baking tray.
Using tongs, return chicken to baking tray and
roast for 5 minutes until sauce is slightly
thickened and sticky.

ONE PAN ROASTS

SIMPLE
SIDES

SILKY MASHED POTATOES

SERVES 4

700g (about 3) Yukon Gold potatoes, peeled and cut
  into 5cm pieces
150ml milk
3 tablespoons unsalted butter
splash of double (thick) cream
sea salt and freshly ground black pepper

Boil potatoes in pan of salted water until
tender to a fork. Meanwhile, gently heat milk
and butter in another pan. Drain potatoes.
Using potato ricer, press potatoes into large
bowl. Pour warm milk mixture over potatoes,
add cream and stir together. Season to taste.

CAULIFLOWER PURÉE

SERVES 4

1 cauliflower, trimmed of leaves and broken into florets
100ml milk
2 tablespoons unsalted butter
sea salt

Place cauliflower in a steamer basket and fill pan with about 5cm water. Steam cauliflower until fork-tender. Drain. Transfer cauliflower to food processor and process with milk and butter, until completely smooth. Season to taste with salt.

CREAMY POLENTA

SERVES 4

150g coarse or medium polenta (cornmeal)
250ml whole milk
60g grated Parmesan cheese
3 tablespoons unsalted butter
sea salt and freshly ground black pepper

Bring 750ml water to the boil. Whisk in
polenta and simmer, stirring occasionally, for
20 minutes. Whisk in milk and continue to
simmer for about 15–20 minutes, stirring
occasionally, until polenta is tender and has
thickened. Stir in Parmesan and butter and
season to taste. Serve immediately.

CLASSIC RISOTTO

SERVES 4

4 tablespoons unsalted butter
2 French shallots, finely chopped
1 garlic clove, very finely chopped
200g Arborio or Carnaroli rice
100ml dry white wine
750ml warm chicken stock
65g grated Parmesan cheese
sea salt and freshly ground black pepper

Melt half the butter in a pan over medium
heat. Add shallots and garlic and cook until
translucent. Add rice and cook, stirring
frequently, for 2–3 minutes. Add wine and
cook, stirring, until almost fully absorbed.
Add 2 ladles of warm stock and stir until
almost fully absorbed. Continue, adding a
ladleful of stock at a time and stirring
constantly, for about 25 minutes until rice is
tender and creamy but retains a slight bite.
Stir in Parmesan and remaining butter and
season to taste.

WILD RICE PILAF

SERVES 4–6

5 tablespoons olive oil
1 onion, finely chopped
100g white basmati rice
100g wild rice
125g pomegranate seeds
50g toasted flaked almonds
1 handful of parsley, finely chopped
sea salt

Heat oil in a frying pan over medium–high heat. Add onion and cook for 10 minutes, stirring occasionally, until edges are browned and onion is tender. Cook both rices separately according to packets. Mix all ingredients together and season to taste.

MIDDLE EASTERN COUSCOUS

SERVES 4

250ml chicken stock
175g couscous
2 tablespoons dried currants
1 teaspoon cumin seeds, toasted
1 preserved lemon, rind only, finely diced
  (flesh discarded)
1 handful of coriander, finely diced

Bring stock to the boil in a small pan with
tight-fitting lid. Add couscous, currants and
cumin seeds, cover pan and remove from heat.
Leave for 5 minutes until stock has fully
absorbed. Fluff with fork. Mix in lemon rind
and coriander.

WARM QUINOA SALAD

SERVES 4–6

200g quinoa (red, white or a mix)
2 tablespoons olive oil
1 onion, finely chopped
50g toasted pine nuts
1 handful of herb sprigs, such as chervil, chives,
  parsley or a mix, finely chopped
sea salt and freshly ground black pepper

Bring 350ml water to the boil in a small pan
with a tight-fitting lid. Add quinoa, cover and
reduce to light simmer. Simmer for 15 minutes
or until quinoa is cooked. Meanwhile, heat
oil over medium–high heat and sauté onion for
10 minutes until translucent and browned at
edges. Mix together quinoa, onion, toasted
pine nuts and herbs. Season to taste and serve
warm or at room temperature.

HERBED FARRO

SERVES 4

200g farro
50g toasted walnuts, chopped
juice of ½ lemon
1 handful of parsley, leaves finely chopped
1 handful of tarragon, leaves finely chopped
1 handful of chives, finely chopped
2 tablespoons olive oil
sea salt and freshly ground black pepper

Bring pan of salted water to the boil. Add farro and simmer for 30 minutes or until tender but still slightly chewy. Drain well and transfer to mixing bowl. Toss with remaining ingredients and season to taste.

Many thanks to Catie Ziller and the whole Marabout team for this great opportunity and wonderful project. Kathy Steer, thank you for your guidance, edits and invaluable input: I could not have asked for a more helpful or attentive editor. Special thanks to Lauren Volo, a beautiful photographer and dear friend. Thanks for your talent, enthusiasm and support. A big thank you to Brianna Ashby: thanks for all of your help and good humour in the kitchen. And to all the food styling ladies in NYC who showed me the kitchen ropes, thank you for your tutelage, support and friendship. Thank you to my husband, Eddie, for his love and support and for being my #1 taste tester. Thank you to my parents, Martha and Steven, my biggest champions, and to my grandmother, Gertrude, for teaching me the importance of a home-cooked meal.

Published in 2017 by Murdoch Books, an imprint of Allen & Unwin
First published in 2016 in France by Marabout

Murdoch Books Australia
83 Alexander Street, Crows Nest NSW 2065
Phone: +61 (0)2 8425 0100
murdochbooks.com.au
info@murdochbooks.com.au

Murdoch Books UK
Ormond House, 26—27 Boswell Street, London WC1N 3JZ
Phone: +44 (0) 20 8785 5995
murdochbooks.co.uk
info@murdochbooks.co.uk

For corporate orders and custom publishing contact our business development team at salesenquiries@murdochbooks.com.au

Publisher: Corinne Roberts
Cover Design: Megan Pigott
Design: Minsk Studio
Editors: Kathy Steer, Jane Price
Photographer: Lauren Volo
Production Manager: Rachel Walsh

Text © Molly Shuster 2017
Photography © Lauren Volo 2017

ISBN 978 1 76052 252 0 Australia
ISBN 978 1 76052 752 5 UK
A cataloguing-in-publication entry is available from the catalogue of the National Library of Australia at nla.gov.au
A catalogue record for this book is available from the British Library

Printed by Hang Tai Printing Company Limited, China